SAINT
PAUL'S
CHURCH OF THE NAZARENE

136 Summer Street
Duxbury MA
02332

Bountiful Blessing
EURASIA

2008-9 NMI
MISSION EDUCATION RESOURCES

❋ ❋ ❋

BOOKS

AFRICA
Where the Decades Still Whisper
by Robert Perry

ASIA-PACIFIC
From the Rising of the Sun
by Brent Cobb

THE CARIBBEAN
A Legacy of Love
by Keith Schwanz

EURASIA
Bountiful Blessing
*by R. Franklin Cook, Gustavo Crocker, Jerald D. Johnson,
and T. W. Schofield*

MEXICO AND CENTRAL AMERICA
A Tapestry of Triumph
by Tim Crutcher

SOUTH AMERICA
A Harvest of Holiness
Compiled by Christian Sarmiento

❋ ❋ ❋

ADULT MISSION EDUCATION RESOURCE BOOK

100 YEARS OF MISSIONS
Editors: Aimee Curtis and Rosanne Bolerjack

Bountiful Blessing

EURASIA

BY
R. FRANKLIN COOK, GUSTAVO CROCKER,
JERALD D. JOHNSON, AND T. W. SCHOFIELD

Nazarene Publishing House
Kansas City, Missouri

Copyright 2008
Nazarene Publishing House

ISBN 978-0-8341-2349-6

Printed in the United States of America

Editor: Aimee Curtis
Cover Design: Kevin Williamson
Inside Design: Sharon Page

10 9 8 7 6 5 4 3 2 1

CONTENTS

PREFACE

When I was invited, as regional director, to write the centennial missions book on the Eurasia Region, I decided I could take one of two approaches: (1) become a historian and do an in-depth research of the history of the Church of the Nazarene in Eurasia—a task that would have taken me years of dedicated work, or (2) involve those who have been part of the history themselves in writing their own historical accounts. I decided for the latter.

The following book is a compilation of the personal experiences of key leaders who have invested their lives in Eurasia and who were willing to chronicle their time as pioneers on this region.

After the introductory chapter, you will read the account of Dr. Jerald Johnson, general superintendent emeritus. His story places us in the European part of the Eurasia Region during the key period of the late 1950s to the late 1960s—the critical time in which the work in Europe was established.

Dr. T. W. Schofield records the initial years of Eurasia as a region of the Church of the Nazarene. It was a privilege to collect his impressions about this short yet significant period when the church formalized its existence on the region—a complicated decision due to the fact that it could not be amalgamated as one "homogeneous" geographical area of the world. In spite of his ill health, Dr. Schofield graciously agreed to share his memories, and his chapter on the years between 1984 and 1989 is valuable to the overall Eurasia story.

The following chapter records the foundational period of the Eurasia Region. A missiologist and writer, Dr. Franklin Cook's contribution to this project is of utmost importance. Dr. Cook gives us a personal account of his tenure as regional director from 1989 to 2004 when the Eurasia Region was established strategically, missiologically, and organizationally. His legacy is still alive and well in the plans and direction of the region today.

Finally, it is my privilege to share some results of my short tenure as regional director since taking office in 2004. As with most leadership succession ventures, the outcomes of my initial years are not necessarily my own accounts, but of those who preceded me. I also have the privilege of sharing the vision the Lord has given us for the future of His church in this part of the world. My prayer is that those who follow us find us worthy of being called *good and faithful servants.*

Gustavo Crocker
Eurasia Regional Director

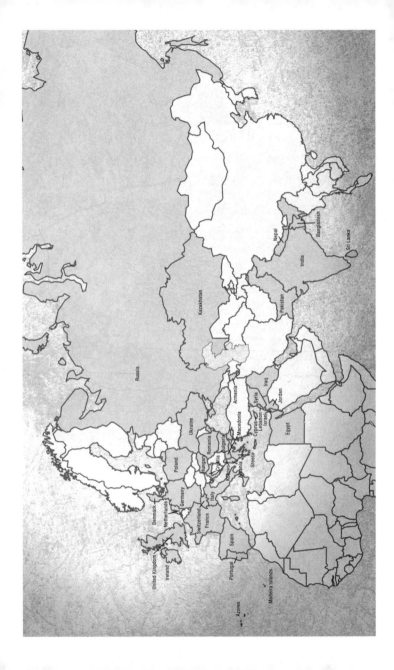

BENVENUE IN EURASIA
The Place Where It All Began
DR. GUSTAVO CROCKER

Welcome to the Eurasia Region, one of the most complex, fascinating, and exciting places to do ministry in the world. This vast region encompasses 93 sovereign nations or distinct areas across Europe, the Middle East, South Asia, North Africa, and the former Soviet Union (also known as the Commonwealth of Independent States—the CIS). This large portion of land covers 14 time zones and encompasses many kinds of religious, cultural, ethnic, and social diversity. More than 2 billion inhabitants of Eurasia speak hundreds of languages and dialects, worship in dozens of religious traditions, utilize scores of currencies for daily economic exchange, and see the world in more perspectives than months in the year.

Dr. Gustavo Crocker

Diversity is the term that best describes the Eurasia Region. It houses 6 of the top 10 developed nations in the world (Norway, Ireland, Iceland, Sweden, Switzerland, and the Netherlands), while a vast majority of South Asian nations live far below poverty lines. Most of the young generations in Western Europe espouse postmodernism while vast areas of the region contain entire communities that are illiterate and premodern.

It is in Eurasia where most of the movements that affect Nazarenes have started over time. A little over 2,000 years ago, Christ was born in a little town located on the region: Bethlehem. He grew up in a place where the Church of the Nazarene today has a vibrant ministry: Nazareth. His words and promises became reality in Jerusalem, Judea, and in Samaria and are now being proclaimed to the ends of the earth.

The missionary work of the apostle Paul also took place entirely in the Eurasia Region. Modern-day Israel, Syria, Lebanon, Turkey, and Greece are countries where he traveled and proclaimed the good news of salvation in Christ during his time.

Centuries later, these countries still remain mission fields needing the message of heart holiness, and the Church of the Nazarene keeps on making disciples where the mission to the Gentiles began.

Not too far from the Eurasia regional office in Büsingen, Germany, are the places where Luther and Zwingli, among others, began the movement to reform Christianity when it had become political and imperialistic. We still can see in this region places where the first Bible was translated and printed for public distribution, as well as other vestiges of a movement that restored access to the gospel by all at all times. Sadly, some of these vestiges are more history than vibrancy, and it is there where the Church of the Nazarene is joining the movement of God to again reform and revive His Church.

> NAZARENES CAN TRACE THEIR DENOMINATIONAL ROOTS TO A SMALL TOWN IN THE EURASIA REGION.

Nazarenes can also trace their denominational roots to a small town in the Eurasia Region. The Wesleyan Methodist movement began less than three centuries ago by a godly man from Epworth, England. Today, John Wesley's teachings have influenced us so much that we Nazarenes claim him as one of the pillars of our theological foundation.

This rich legacy, however, is often contrasted by

the enormous challenge of the diverse religious environment of Eurasia. This region is home to several of the major world religions including Islam, Judaism, Buddhism, and Hinduism, providing many challenges in presenting the clear message of Christ.

The Church of the Nazarene in Eurasia

Inspired by the love of Christ, the Church of the Nazarene is committed to proclaiming the message of His salvation in spite of challenges and complexities. We are doing this through established ministries in 39 nations divided into six strategic fields. From the denomination's first mission field in India, begun in 1898, to the newest fields in Kosovo and Iraq, started in 2005, we offer medical services; food and clothing for the orphaned; relief for refugees from wars, ethnic cleansing, and natural disasters; education at all levels; and important spiritual nurturing through the work of more than 1,000 local churches.

Each field on the region is responsible for facilitating the work of the Church of the Nazarene in their respective nations and/or districts. For the most part, ministry is facilitated by missionaries (volunteer and contracted) but the bulk of the implementation of ministry is in the hands of capable Eurasians who carry the daily tasks of the Kingdom in their communities. The six fields of the Eurasia Region are as follows:

- **CIS Field:** Begun in the early 1990s, this field covers the nations of the former Soviet Union. The Church of the Nazarene has ministries in Ukraine, Russia, Kazakhstan, Armenia, and several creative access nations. Most of the work in this field has been in existence for 15 years or less.

- **Eastern Mediterranean Field:** This field covers the Middle East. The Church of the Nazarene has established ministries in Israel, Jordan, Egypt, Syria, Cyprus, Lebanon, and several creative access nations. Most of the work in this field has been in existence for over 50 years, however new works in areas like Iraq make this field a combination of pioneer and established work.

- **Northern European Field:** This field includes the Northwestern portion of Europe. The Church of the Nazarene has established ministries in Ireland, England, Scotland, Wales, Northern Ireland, the Netherlands, Denmark, Norway, Poland, Germany, Switzerland, and Hungary. This field is home to some of the earliest expressions of the holiness movement as well as some of the newest works of the Church of the Nazarene. In fact, in this field we find works that predate the foundation of the Church of the Nazarene (Scotland) and fields that have less than 15 years of existence (Poland, Hungary).

- **South Asia Field:** The largest in membership (85 percent), this field covers the South Asian subcontinent. The Church of the Nazarene has ministries in India (the oldest missionary field of the denomination), Pakistan, Bangladesh, Nepal, and Sri Lanka.

• **Southeastern European Field:** The youngest in the region, the Southeastern European Field (SEE) covers most of the Balkans, Eastern Europe, and the Central Mediterranean. In existence since the early 1990s, the church has ministries in Albania, Bulgaria, Romania, Macedonia, Slovenia, and Kosovo. Also included in this field are Greece and Croatia. The only work in this field that is part of the early European ministry is Italy, in existence for nearly 50 years.

• **Western Mediterranean Field:** Catholic and Muslim in background, this field covers the Iberian Peninsula and Northern Africa. The Church of the Nazarene has been present in this field for nearly 30 years and has work in France, Spain, Portugal, the Azores, and the Madeira Islands.

These six fields are now developed structures in the missionary enterprise of the Church of the Nazarene in Eurasia. Reaching this point, however, required sacrifice on the part of missionaries and national leaders who spent their lives sharing the gospel. Many lost their lives while their work suffered incredible setbacks due to the hardness of the soil in this part of the world. While this book cannot adequately tell the story of each saint whose life has been invested in transforming Eurasia "in Christ, like Christ, for Christ," the following pages will give personal accounts of a few servant leaders who have been instrumental in the development of the Eurasia Region over the last few decades.

BEFORE BOLTON
The Beginning of the Work in Europe
DR. JERALD D. JOHNSON

In 1958 the Church of the Nazarene celebrated its 50th anniversary. In recognition of this fact, a decision was made to expand into two new countries: Brazil and Germany. My wife and I were selected for the latter assignment, and our arrival in Germany began a long and lasting love affair with Europe.

Political Environment in Europe

We settled into our new home in Frankfurt just as the Cold War was beginning to heat up. While considerable rebuilding had taken place since the end of World War II, much remained to be done. In many places debris still laid piled up in areas where large buildings had once stood. Housing was difficult to find as many people still lived in makeshift shelters. Rebuilding was the order of the day—not just physical rebuilding, but political restructuring as well.

Communism was also still a threat. Driving

through what then, of necessity, came to be known as West Germany we observed missiles aimed toward the east. We were confident that in the east there were missiles aimed toward the west. One of our greatest concerns was that one side or the other might get "trigger-happy."

Dr. Jerald D. Johnson

When the wall in Berlin was built, tensions mounted to a feverish pitch. I recall seeing tanks parked behind a building just a block or so away from the wall on the western side. That their motors were idling, ready to move out, was of no particular comfort to me.

We observed other barriers as well. From the north to south, all along the border between East and West Germany, the Soviets with their East German allies had built a nearly foolproof fence barrier. This made it practically impossible for anyone to escape. A few did, but many more lost their lives. Guards, land mines, vicious dogs, and other ugly obstacles dotted what under normal circumstances was, or should have been, a beautiful landscape of meadows and luscious forests.

A barrier was also erected around the entire city of Berlin making travel into the once proud capital city of Germany very difficult. As a result, it became impossible for Berlin to serve the country as the seat of government. Therefore the city of Bonn in the West became a temporary capital city. The Germans were always quick to refer to Bonn as just that, their *temporary* capital. They dreamed and planned for the day their country would be reunified.

Religion in Europe

In 1517 a German monk by the name of Martin Luther openly protested certain practices of his own Roman Catholic Church. This resulted in the Reformation, which brought about the establishment of Protestantism. The movement spread quickly as nobles, peasants, and townspeople joined in the protests. Because of this, they became known as Protestants, and the name has remained to this day.

The Catholic Church subsequently underwent its own reform called the Counter Reformation. Through this they won back many Protestants, but not always by peaceful means. The result was that by 1600 few Protestants remained in Austria, Bavaria, parts of Bohemia, and the Rhineland region of Germany.

The Reformation soon moved into other areas of Europe—such as England, Scotland, and Wales—where Protestant churches are predominant. Other countries remain predominately Catholic, such as France and Italy.

When we entered Germany with the Church of the Nazarene in 1958 we experienced this interesting division of Protestant and Catholic churches first-hand. Lutheran, Protestant churches were by this time identified as Evangelisch (Evangelical) State Churches. But Catholic churches, although not so named, were for all practical purposes state churches as well. Both groups were supported by a tax system collected through a payroll deduction method.

Following the war, support of the churches—not just with taxes but also with attendance—became rather intense. While food, housing, and other necessities were in short supply, the people appeared to be faithful to their churches. It was often said that when Germany's garbage cans were empty, their churches were full. There came a time, however, when the nation began to right itself economically and the reverse became true. When their garbage cans were full, the churches sat empty—or at least considerably less full than before.

Where did the Church of the Nazarene fit into this picture? First of all it is important to note that while there had been a surge in church attendance following World War II, this represented only a small percentage of the membership of the two large denominational churches. And as life began to progress following the war, many people left their church. Both Catholics and Protestants experienced large declines in membership. In order to be taken off the rolls it was necessary to go to an official office of the state and make the request, but always the request was granted. This in turn relieved people of paying the church tax.

The Church of the Nazarene fits into the category of what is called an Evangelical free church. "Free" simply means it is not a part of the state church system and for that reason does not receive church taxes. Upon our arrival, we rather naively thought we would simply find our place in the larger church community and find acceptance among the free churches. This, however, didn't play out as we thought. The free churches have an organization known as the Free Church Alliance. Initially we were not accepted by this alliance, nor did we get the impression that we ever would be. And we felt the two large state church organizations, the Catholics and the Protestants, looked upon us as intruders into their territory.

Because German cities were divided into parishes, any property we purchased automatically placed us in another church's territory. In our area of Frankfurt, we found our purchase had placed us in areas assigned to a large Protestant church to the east and a Catholic church to the west. Not far from us was also a seminary belonging to one of the free churches. That is where we experienced the first resistance to our denomination. A leading professor from that seminary came to our home for a visit. I sincerely thought I had found a friend with whom I could experience fellowship, and thus I looked upon him as my brother in the faith. He pointedly asked me what I would be preaching. I identified myself as a Wesleyan theologically and emphasized our cardinal doctrine of holiness. I spoke of sanctification as a second work of grace, carefully trying to use Wesleyan terms. I was shocked at his response. "I forbid you," he said, "I forbid you to preach that in Germany." I'm sure he felt he was a final authority on the subject and had the right to dictate the message I could preach. However, as a part of Germany's postwar constitution, religious freedom had been assured. This meant I could preach what I chose, and it further meant our church had every right to exist and minister in the country.

Our intrusion into Protestant and Catholic territory became an issue at a later time as well. The nearby state Protestant church became especially concerned when they realized we fully intended to construct a church building on the land we purchased. An invitation was extended for my wife and me to visit their church board with not only the parish pastor being present, but also their dekan (comparable to a district superintendent) presiding over the session. They wanted to inquire who we were and why we were there. Our evening with them was something like being grilled in cross examination by a prosecuting attorney. I wanted to have the last word as I had made up my mind we would extend an olive branch that might be difficult for them to refuse.

I began by asking them how many members they had in their local congregation. They responded with 10,000. I then asked what their average attendance was. They said it was about 300. Before I could make the same suggestion, one of the board members spoke up and suggested that perhaps it would be all right for us to try to minister to the other 9,700. I then asked the dekan if, once our church was constructed, he would be willing to come and preach a sermon in our church. It was not the kind of request he anticipated, and a few embarrassing moments followed when another board member suggested that perhaps I could come and preach from their pulpit sometime.

No actual invitation was forthcoming and no dates were set, but I felt we had at least built a

SOME WEEKS LATER A FEW MEMBERS OF MY CHURCH SHOWED ME A PAMPHLET THAT HAD BEEN DISTRIBUTED TO OUR NEIGHBORHOOD. IT WAS A WARNING FOR PEOPLE NOT TO ATTEND THE NAZARENE CHURCH.

bridge between us. Much to my surprise, however, some weeks later a few members of my church showed me a pamphlet that had apparently been distributed to each household in our neighborhood. It was a warning for people not to attend the Nazarene church. It was signed by the pastor and dekan of the Protestant church and the priest of the local Catholic church. I did not let this go unchallenged. I called both churches, spoke to their ministers, and expressed my disappointment in them. I had sincerely felt we would not be in competition but would simply enhance their ministries by our presence. They obviously felt otherwise. It did not affect us negatively, however. In fact a bit of "persecution" seemed to light the fire of our small congregation a bit brighter and became an incentive to work harder. Even then, it was our desire to be friends. I felt we had too much respect for our Christian heritage to be anything else.

After my family and I left and returned to the United States in 1969, I learned the professor from the nearby seminary began to attend our church quite regularly. Also, the big news in the state Protestant church parish was that the dekan experienced a definite born-again experience. He testified to it and became a changed man with kinder attitudes and a genuine Christian spirit.

The day finally came when our church was not just accepted into the Alliance of Free Churches, but became an active part of it. Furthermore our pastors occasionally receive invitations to preach in state Protestant churches while pastors from their churches have preached in ours. It is of special significance that several state church pastors have experienced a new birth in Christ, thus infusing new life and spiritual vitality into the Protestant movement.

Workers for the Harvest

There came a day in our ministry in Europe when we learned why Jesus said we were to pray to the Lord of the harvest to send workers into the harvest. It was never intended that a flood of missionaries would be sent to the European continent. Rather, from the beginning, it was assumed necessary laborers would be found from the various countries to minister to their own people. Britain provided a model of what should be done on the continent. British preachers have always commanded our admiration and, without question, some of the greatest spiritual leaders and preachers, not to mention missionaries, have come from the British Isles. If that could happen there, then why not on the other side of the English Channel as well?

In the beginning days of our work in Germany, we were blessed with friendly relations with The

Salvation Army. Help from them, for example, was secured for some of our translating needs. One of their officers and his wife even felt compelled to seek the blessing of their superiors to make the switch to the Church of the Nazarene and assist us in our work. This wonderful couple, recently retired, provided us with invaluable service over the years.

We were blessed time and time again as God responded to our prayer for workers in unique and wonderful ways. There were those who were converted in our churches and then felt the call to pre-

European Nazarene College

pare for ministry. Some young people, not previously Nazarenes, attended European Nazarene Bible College (now European Nazarene College) and received their calls while studying there. I look back upon our ministry and marvel how God creatively took care of our needs.

Soon it wasn't just Germany that needed Nazarene ministers. The day came when we needed someone to minister in the Netherlands too. In fact it was a desperate need. A group of Dutch Christians, friends of Jeannine van Beek, requested I meet with them in one of their small-group Bible studies in Haarlem, Holland. They had many questions about the Church of the Nazarene, and I enjoyed my fellowship with them immensely. Soon they asked about becoming a part of the Church of the Nazarene, offering to be a core group for beginning the denomination in their country. After organizing them into a church body, we began searching for a pastor. In the meantime I was the titular pastor until we secured permanent leadership.

I could not meet with them often as it was a rather long distance from our home in Frankfurt, Germany. I drove over to be with them about every four to five weeks. At that time I received from them the rather dubious title of being their "Flying Dutchman."

We prayed earnestly for a Dutch-speaking pastor who would be willing to help these folks pioneer the work in their country. Finally, it appeared we had a fine brother ready to come. He was a native of the Netherlands and now a missionary in our church. Upon making his own earnest search to know God's will for his ministry, however, he felt compelled to remain in missionary work. Of course we respected his decision, but were admittedly disappointed. It was with a heavy heart that I made the journey to Haarlem to inform the little group we had to move back to point zero in our search.

Little did I know what God was preparing for us, however. One of the lovely couples in the core group was a gentleman by the name of Cor Holleman and his wife, Miep. Their enthusiasm for the work had already proven to be contagious, and they were attracting other good people to our group.

When I arrived in Haarlem to bring the discouraging news that we had no pastor, Cor took me to the side. He told me he had made an agreement with the Lord that if I came and had no pastor for them, this would be a sign he was to give up his job and prepare for ministry in the Church of the Nazarene. When Cor shared this with me I had an immediate response in my own heart, which of course was very positive. As I look back on it now, I recall I found myself almost in disbelief that such a wonderful answer had been found.

Cor Holleman

Cor went on to become a successful pastor and later became the first national district superintendent in the Netherlands. He led the church through successful periods of growth. Today, the work of the Church of the Nazarene in that country is one of our brightest spots in the denomination.

God continued to work in marvelous ways in response to our prayer for workers in Germany. At the conclusion of World War II, a young man named Richard turned 18 years old and made a decision to step out on his own. The war had left him disillusioned and even angry. His experiences growing up in wartime Germany had been negative ones. This was compounded by what he felt was unfair treatment his father had received as an officer in the German army. His decision led him to emigrate from Germany to South Africa.

In South Africa, Richard met a young lady whose mother happened to be a charter member of one of our European churches in South Africa. Dr. Charles Strickland had been sent by the Church of the Nazarene to pioneer this work among the Europeans in South Africa.

30

I met up with Dr. Strickland at the 1960 General Assembly, and we shared experiences with one another. In the course of conversation he told me he had a contact who he felt might help us with our ministerial needs in Germany. He then told me about Richard Zanner who was now married and wonderfully converted. Conversion had not come easy for Richard, though. He had taken delight in arguing religion with his mother-in-law. The kind of religion she had was not for him, he insisted. However, upon her death he came across a little book in which she kept her prayer requests. There he found his name underscored as a particular concern. This discovery made its way into Richard's heart, and it wasn't long afterward that he made his way to a Church of the Nazarene and gave his heart to God.

The two men became friends. Dr. Strickland obviously looked upon Richard as the apostle Paul did young Timothy. It soon became clear that Richard did indeed have gifts for ministry and felt inclined to respond to what seemed to be the call of God. Our Bible college—then located in Johannesburg, South Africa—beckoned Richard, and he began theological studies there.

Richard and his wife now had two little girls, so he had to work to support his family and attend classes on the side. In school, under the tutorship of Dr. Floyd Perkins, Richard began to hear the message of holiness. Discussion of what took place in the classes occupied the time Richard had with his mentor, Dr. Strickland. At the same time, God was speaking to Richard, and he found himself under genuine conviction. He finally stood up in class and asked his fellow students and professor to pray that he might be sanctified holy. The entire class knelt in prayer, and it was not long until Richard Zanner stood to testify that God had given him a clean heart and filled him with the Holy Spirit.

Dr. Strickland now felt Richard was ready to serve in Europe. A short time later, however, Richard received distressing news from Germany. His father, now a victim of cancer, was not expected to live.

Richard and Valerie Zanner

Richard's love for his father compelled him to travel to Germany as quickly as possible in order to win his dad to the Lord.

When Richard arrived in his hometown, I received a telegram from Dr. Strickland telling me that the young man of whom he had spoken was now in Germany. I immediately made contact with Richard and invited him to Frankfurt so we could get acquainted with one another.

Our meeting concluded with me telling him it would be wonderful if he didn't have to return to Africa, but rather stay in his native Germany and serve the Lord there. He said he would pray about it and would be in contact with his wife over the matter. A few days later Richard called to say he would stay, but he would have to find a way to bring his wife and two daughters from Africa to join him.

At that time we had a group of servicemen and their families meeting on Sunday afternoons for English church services. I called these servicemen our "missionaries in uniform," reminding them God had a purpose for them being stationed in Germany. I went to this group of servicemen and told them about the results of my visit with Richard. "Would you be willing," I asked, "to raise the money to bring this man's wife and two little girls to Germany?" They accepted the challenge, and in a short while we had enough money to make the trip possible.

When my wife and I returned to the United States in 1969, the district elected Richard Zanner the first German district superintendent. He served quite well in this capacity until 1980. At that time, I was serving as the director of World Mission when the Board of General Superintendents asked if together we could convince Richard to return to Africa. He would initially serve as superintendent of the European District there, but at the same time begin setting up what would become our first regional office outside of the United States. After one or two years he would then become regional director. Richard accepted the assignment and set the machinery in motion for racial integration of our churches in South Africa. This was eventually accomplished under his leadership as regional director.

Twenty years later Richard Zanner retired as regional director and minister in the Church of the Nazarene. When he took on the African assignment in 1980 there were approximately 30,000 Nazarenes on the continent. At the time of his retirement there were about 130,000 Nazarenes. God had used him in a marvelous way.

Is this a testimonial argument for Europe being considered a missional must? Is it also an argument for God's people to follow the admonition of our Lord to pray for workers for the harvest? The challenges are immense, but the opportunities are also immense. May we as Nazarenes be faithful to do what God expects of us. If we take the necessary steps of faith, He will provide the means to fulfill His purposes.

FROM BOLTON
TO BERLIN
Setting the Scene

DR. T. W. SCHOFIELD

Before becoming the first regional director for what is now the Eurasia Region, I had served the Church of the Nazarene largely in the European sphere for almost 40 years. Twenty-four of those years I pastored five different churches, all of which reported growth, and then I served 15 years as the second district superintendent of the British Isles South District. During this period I was also elected twice to serve on the General Board of the Church of the Nazarene. The second period I served on the World Mission General Board Committee. At this point in time Dr. L. Guy Nees, director of World Mission, also supervised the Europe/Middle East Region while the other regions had their own directors in place.

My involvement in regional coordination (and later, direction) happened as a result of two property-purchasing visits to Southern Europe. A proposed property purchase in Madrid was under way and running into some difficulties. The owner had visited with Nazarene leaders at our denominational headquarters to resolve the issues, but to little avail. Dr. Nees asked if I would fly to Spain and determine if a solution was feasible. He told me they had agreed to have a

Dr. T. W. Schofield

banker's draft in Madrid in seven days. After much negotiation, we met the deadline and purchased the property. Dr. Nees described the speed of this purchase as a modern miracle.

One miracle deserves another, so a request was made for me to travel to Portugal and provide advice on another property-purchase issue there. While discussions were still ongoing, the government in Portugal devalued the *escudo*—their local currency. The result was that we were able, with the same amount of money, to purchase the original property as well as property for a second church in another area. Talk about miracles!

After these trips to Southern Europe, the pace quickened. Dr Nees asked if I would be willing to serve as regional coordinator for the Europe/Middle East Region along with my role as superintendent of the British Isles South District. The Board of General Superintendents agreed to go ahead for one year if the South District agreed. This they did, and one of my pastors—Rev. L. H. McNeil—helped lighten my load by acting as my district business manager.

The question of locating a regional office and staffing it soon arose. Since I was already 62 years old, I was told I could remain in Britain and travel from there as needed. An international airport in Manchester, only 30 minutes from my home in Bolton, helped facilitate my travel. I was then able to purchase an affordable piece of property and employ both full- and part-time staff. Shortly thereafter my secretary in the district office, Mrs. Joan Barnes, and Rev. John Haines came aboard with three other part-time staff. We were on our way. Soon a volunteer facilities consultant and an assistant coordinator joined us, and we began shaping what turned out to be the first regional office for the Church of the Nazarene in Eurasia.

The conviction that local church leaders and district leaders should now move together to make situations more harmonious was not an easy pill for everyone to swallow. However, we focused our attempts in this direction. We held our first regional conference and made regular visits to most of the countries in the Europe/Middle East Region.

Soon we began an outreach to the Azores with

the help of Dr. and Mrs. Earl Mosteller and pursued contacts in Egypt. Unfortunately, we encountered problems with leadership and motivation in Egypt. As a result, we organized several gatherings in various cities to help ease tensions. These visits seemed promising even though we were chased by the Secret Police and detained in customs in Cairo. Makram Bessada was the local person who provided leadership in this country.

> POLICE AND MILITARY BECAME INVOLVED AS A CROWD OF ABOUT 2,000 PEOPLE TRIED TO BREAK INTO THE SCHOOL WHERE WE HAD GATHERED OUR PEOPLE.

The Work in the Middle East

The Holy Land had always been a difficult field since commencement in 1921, and recruiting suitable pastoral leadership proved to be extremely difficult. Again more excitement was on its way. We held a camp in a rented school near Bethlehem with about 80 to 90 people present. I was speaking, and we saw good results with people finding the Lord. On the last day, however, altercations between youth in our camp and village boys eventually culminated in a riot. Police and military became involved as a crowd of about 2,000 people tried to break into the school where we had gathered our people. But God's hand and protection kept us safe.

Nazarene Theological College

This seemed to spark a holy fire among our young people, and I believe some are still in the ministry with us today. Consequently, we soon built new facilities in Nazareth for educational work.

While the work in Lebanon was difficult, we continued to make steady progress. We rented the Bible school property in Beirut to a university, and this income helped finance a new church in Karak, Jordan. Rev. Jacob Ammari provided excellent leadership, helping to establish Sunday Schools in Ramallah and other places.

The need for educating young students was paramount, so we looked for property to purchase in a neutral area. We decided on Cyprus and soon began a summer school program with students from

Israel, Jordan, Lebanon, and Egypt. Personnel from British Isles Nazarene College (now Nazarene Theological College) gave of their time to teach in the school. Funding to purchase the property came from a group in California, and Dr. L. Guy Nees was present at the opening exercises.

New Challenges

During my time as regional director our budget was small, and this did, to some extent, limit the growth of the region. The next surprise came when India was added to the region and the name was changed to the Eurasia Region. Of course British influence had been paramount for many years in India, and the work there developed well.

Eventually missionary levels dropped in India due to retirement and strict government regulations regarding new visas. This meant missionaries going on furlough were not allowed back into India. While disappointing, this development gave the denomination the opportunity to utilize national workers in leadership. Although India had been the first mission field of the Church of the Nazarene, membership stood at only 5,000 to 6,000 by the mid-1980s. Within a couple of years of national leadership, these numbers increased more than tenfold. Reynolds Memorial Hospital—opened some 40 years prior—as well as a nursing college and Bible school had also

Reynolds Memorial Hospital

flourished in Washim largely under missionary leadership. Their vision, however, was to seek full national leadership among both doctors and staff. As a result, this work still prospers today. Names like Dr. V. J. Singh, Dr. C. S. Dahs, Rev. Dinakaran, Rev. Gaikwad, and Rev. Ingle evoke memories of faithful leadership in transition.

Poland and Beyond

In south Poland, tentative plans to share in a medical center failed to materialize while I was regional director. Years later, however, long after my departure, these plans and seeds came to fruition, and it is now wonderful to see Poland beginning to open up to the gospel.

With political changes in Europe and the demolition of the Berlin Wall, the stage was set for greater cohesion among the nations. The time for my retirement was also quickly approaching, and I was happy to learn Dr. Cook would replace me. Unfortunately, my retirement was jump-started in a way with a scorpion bite in Egypt that led to deep vein thrombosis and severe spinal problems.

Since then my contact with the Eurasia Region has

City center in Poznan, Poland

continued, and I have always felt honored to have had this opportunity to serve the Savior and the church I love so much. Now housebound and under daily supervision, I still feel so spiritually and mentally wrapped up in Eurasia. To adequately put pen to paper is a near impossibility, but I hope these memories will be of help and praise to our Redeemer.

FROM BERLIN TO BAGHDAD
The Establishment of the Eurasia Region

DR. R. FRANKLIN COOK

It was the middle of the night, and I was in the Middle East. I was restless from mild jetlag and thoughts of the district assembly in Jordan. The day had been eventful, and sleep was not coming easily.

Sleeplessness led to flipping on the television and tuning in CNN International for the latest news. Unanticipated, I began to witness pictures coming from Berlin—history live on television. At 10:30 P.M. on November 9, 1989, guards were forced to open the border gates between East and West Berlin, and shortly after, thousands gathered and began to chip at the notorious Berlin Wall.

Sleep was now out of the question.

That wall had been constructed in 1961 and had divided the great city of Berlin all the years that followed. It was the scourge that represented a division of peoples, families, values, political systems, superpowers, and even cultures. Hundreds had been killed in an attempt to climb over, float over, or dig under the wall, or execute numerous other innovative ways to breach the barrier. It was where presidents John F. Kennedy and Ronald Reagan had made dramatic appearances and speeches. And at Checkpoint Charlie, American and Soviet tanks had faced each other gun barrel to gun barrel waiting for the order to start World War III.

Dr. Franklin Cook

As I lay in my Jordan bed watching, I knew the world was about to change. In addition, I had this foreboding feeling that my job was about to change—dramatically. I had only been regional director of the Eurasia Region for a mere five weeks. Boxes of my move were still packed and stacked in a borrowed apartment in Germany. And now this!

My first response as regional director was a call for what became known as a "Berlin Summit." This was a gathering at a Christian retreat center in West Berlin of people representing the International Headquarters of the Church of the Nazarene and other individuals representing significant potential resources. By the time we had all gathered—along with the pastors in Berlin and the district superin-

tendent of the German District, Thomas Vollenwei-
der—we represented youth, literature, radio, World
Mission, Sunday School, Compassionate Ministries,
and several other ministries including large local
churches in the United States.

As our group of about 30 spent nearly a week
together, we prayed, discussed, and debated what
this new reality meant. What did it mean for the
Eurasia Region and for the Church of the Nazarene?
What would it require to gather money, missionaries, and resources to begin thinking about places the
church had never been? We at least knew it would
mean new languages, cultures, economies, and strate-
gies. We walked the streets of Berlin, talked to people, saw several compassionate ministry centers
already in progress, dreamed, and planned.

We had many things to accomplish. In many
ways this represented what would happen on the
entire Eurasia Region in the near future. We had to
create a mission statement, focus our attention on
how to plant healthy and lasting churches in brand-
new areas, and train indigenous personnel to carry the
message and ministries of a holiness denomination.

We had to figure out our priorities, and we had
to do it fast. Hundreds of volunteers, individually
and in groups, began to flood into Eastern Europe
and the former Soviet Union, which was in the
process of dissolving. Teams representing colleges,

universities, and local churches began to hook on to interests in these places. Simply put, it was not even organized chaos; it was just chaos.

Finally, we had to gather resources from every possible sector of the denomination. In doing so, we made a wonderful discovery. Individuals with warm hearts and active in their faith responded generously. We began to receive gifts, money, and people beyond our expectations.

In the early years of my tenure, it became obvious the Eurasia Region fell into three noncompatible subregions: South Asia, the Middle East, and Europe. As time moved forward, however, we found things were more complicated than this. Europe alone suggests northern, southern, central, and Eastern Europe, and even that doesn't describe its reality. The ministry in the United Kingdom is unique. The Balkans has its own flair and flavor. The Middle East has swirling interests and conflicts. There are political conflicts inside South Asia.

In God's

Hermann and Brigitte Gschwandtner

timing and with His guidance, an effective leadership team came together to make things happen. For example, Dr. Hermann Gschwandtner, a German pastor who had worked for years in a parachurch European mission agency, offered himself to become the first eastern European coordinator. Hermann, who is something of a tornadic force himself, was everywhere at the same time, meeting people, organizing registrations of the denomination, and gathering resources. Coming from a culture that has a guttural response to new situations of "this is impossible," Hermann represented the new thinking "of course we can do this." Together we made most things work.

Over time we began to find missionary staff to assist with opening the work in country after country. The generosity of people in the form of regular tithes, giving to the World Evangelism Fund, and extra mission donations enabled us to support the rapidly expanding ministries in both old and new areas.

In looking at the years that followed—the "Berlin to Baghdad" years (1989 to 2004)—I believe they can be summarized this way:

1. <u>Finding the mission.</u> First we found a collective way, as a group of Nazarenes, to express what our mission, goals, and purpose were. It is not enough to win people to Christ. The call is to disciple and create expressions of the Body of Christ that

will be the agency of nurture and spiritual growth. Across the region, we had to find this mission.

2. <u>Entering new countries.</u> When the Berlin Wall came down and the Soviet Union dissolved, we saw at least 25 new nations as possibilities for the Church of the Nazarene. Each one was completely different. They had different laws governing the work of churches, especially evangelical churches. Every new country entered could fill the pages of its individual book.

3. <u>Establishing the identity.</u> Finally, our corporate task was not just to do good things—although a myriad of good things were done. It was to establish the Church of the Nazarene. What is unique in our doctrine, polity and governance, and culture that identifies a Nazarene in Bulgaria, or Armenia, or Bangladesh? That was an intense and ongoing conversation.

PEOPLE ACROSS THE EURASIA REGION WHO HAD FALLEN INTO THE COMPLACENCY OF THEIR NORMAL CHRISTIAN LIVES WERE SHAKEN LOOSE AND CHALLENGED TO FIND NEW WAYS OF "DOING CHURCH."

Europe was in the throes of dramatic change, such as the reunification of Germany in October of 1990. Things were also happening in other parts of the region, however. By August of 1990 it was obvious the Middle East was again to have a major war. Iraq had invaded Kuwait, and through the remaining months there was a buildup to the eventual invasion of Iraq in 1991. It took just six weeks for a coalition of forces to crush Iraq and free Kuwait.

This had a dramatic effect on the work of Nazarenes in the Middle East. Suddenly centers of power shifted. Thousands of Iraqi refugees poured into Jordan. The Church of the Nazarene responded in a positive demonstration of Christ's love and compassion. Several churches in the Jordanian capitol of Amman aggressively entered Iraqi refugee camps with bundles of food, clothing, and blankets funded by Nazarene Compassionate Ministries. In addition, they included portions of Scripture or entire Bibles in Arabic along with contact information and invitations to church.

Finding the Mission

People across the Eurasia Region who had fallen into the complacency of their normal Christian lives were shaken loose and challenged to find new ways of "doing church." Every time we had a leadership meeting—whether regionally, on the district level, or in a local church—we rehearsed these basic questions. What is your mission? What is God calling you to do? What is God saying in this turbulent world?

One of the emerging organizations on the region was Nazarene Youth International (NYI). Ms. Deidre

Members of NYI in Europe

Brower was appointed youth coordinator and immediately began to organize groups of young people across the region in retreats, small groups, coalitions, and congresses for times of worship, preaching, and teaching. Eventually her work was recognized by the denomination when Deidre was elected general NYI president and as such became a member of the General Board of the denomination. Out of the youth organization came a number of emerging leaders.

Entering New Countries

There was a time in the history of the Church of the Nazarene when we entered

Deidre Brower

new countries one by one, in an orderly manner, and usually supported by a major fundraising offering. Such was the case in Papua New Guinea, Venezuela, and Germany. All of this happened many years ago. But now there was a flood of need, and open doors beckoned in every direction. From 1989 and for the next decade, there was no "neat and tidy" way to open countries. We did it any way we could, and no two had the same story.

In some cases we entered through Compassionate Ministry activity by meeting a crisis. In other cases we discovered people who migrated from one area to another in this new and almost borderless world and had carried the church with them. At least the Iron Curtain had disappeared. In still other cases students from various countries had heard of the Church of the Nazarene and had come to learn at a Nazarene educational institution, such as European Nazarene College or Nazarene Theological College in England. Often it became a natural thing for graduates, now Nazarene, to desire to return to their own countries and begin the work of the church there.

We soon began to learn important lessons most people do not consider. For example, every country has its own set of laws. In some countries no new denominations were allowed to enter and register without a minimum number of members. How do you have members *before* you arrive? These numbers also ranged from 100 to 100,000. We had to find ways around these regulations and still not break any national laws.

Some countries only had a limited number of official denominations and were not allowing new ones to be added. Usually these denominations predated communist times and had their roots a century or longer. Newcomers were not welcomed.

How do you acquire property for a church where there are no laws governing the purchase of private property? Remember that under communism there was no such thing as private property; everything was owned by the state. Or, in other cases, only 99-year-leases on land were available. Creative thinking found ways to acquire property and buildings for ministry.

Suspicion of a new church was rampant. We were called a cult in many places. In other areas, the Orthodox Church opposed any Evangelical church and fought its recognition. Who were these Nazarenes anyway?

Establishing the Identity

Once a foothold was gained, we then had to establish our identity. In many ways this was the hardest step of all. We began by putting together groups of diverse people—mixing veteran Nazarenes with new Nazarenes as much as possible. In addition to the important work of NYI in this regard, we also had a Regional Advisory Council that met annually to make regional decisions. We reconfigured this council in a number of ways as we experimented with the most effective kind of group to put together.

We also held two regional conferences between Berlin and Baghdad as an opportunity to bring together a larger number of people, usually around 300, in one place for a week of preaching, inspiration, vision casting, and teaching.

Then there were the groups that came out of district development, such as the Advisory Board, and other special events that brought clergy and laity together. Leadership conferences, many sponsored by our educational institutions, provided tremendous forums for establishing identity. In addition to this, we created ad hoc groups to study specific projects, such as strategy, self-support, or leadership. In each case, people from different regional areas had the opportunity to study together and work out problems.

We soon began to adopt a principle Rev. Chuck Sunberg, pioneer missionary to the former Soviet Union, used on his field. He called it the "square one" principle. Soon we were all talking about the importance of square one. This meant every time we got together we talked again about the Church of the Nazarene, how we started, where we came from, what we believe and why, our mission statement, and where we were going. This mantra was repeated so often that emerging leaders could quote the speech by memory. Identity is a key ingredient to having a healthy organization.

As mentioned earlier, areas of the region other than Europe were experiencing dramatic change as well. South Asia was in the throes of emerging from a postcolonial period and entering a new and flattened world where every voice could be heard.

South Asia is a compacted part of the world including the Indian subcontinent; adjoining nations near the Himalayan mountain range; and nearby Islands, such as Sri Lanka, the Maldives, and others. The Indian subcontinent was at one time the nation of India, but following the convulsion of independence in 1947-1948, it was partitioned into what became Bangladesh and Pakistan.

When I arrived as regional director, I found correspondence in the files including a letter from Mr. Li Fuamui, a Samoan Nazarene who held a high post with the United Nations. Mr. Faumui was stationed in the capitol of Bangladesh as head of the development office. He was conducting a Bible study in his home and invited the Church of the Nazarene to come to Bangladesh to explore the possibilities of opening work. I was eager to take him up on his offer.

Dr. Steve Weber, director of Nazarene Compassionate Ministries at the time, made a dramatic trip to South Asia with me in 1991. There we were hosted by Mr. Faumui and some of his key contacts.

During a long afternoon at the Faumui house, a group of approximately 30 Bangladeshi leaders who were in the Bible study came together to meet Steve and me. We asked questions. They asked questions. We discussed the Church of the Nazarene and explained who we were and what we believed. Our desire was to determine whether the church should enter this part of the world once again, after being absent for 60 years.

After the meeting, Steve and I returned to the hotel and a few hours later I received a telephone call. It was Sukumal Biswas, another member of the Bible study. He was in the lobby of the hotel asking if he could meet with us. Steve and I were delighted and spent another several hours with Sukumal talking about the Church of the Nazarene.

The end result was that Sukumal, who had worked with the Bible Society of Bangladesh and Food for the Hungry, became our leader and remains so today. After registering the Church of the Nazarene both as a church and as a compassionate ministry entity (an NGO, nongovernmental organization), the work began, and the results have been dramatic. Bangladesh has become one of the rapid growing districts in the Church of the Nazarene.

Meantime, in Pakistan, a process began that eventually brought Alexander Roberts to the Church of the Nazarene as a leader. As a young man Alexander traveled from Pakistan to work in the oil industry in Libya, in North Africa, and became a believing Christian as the result of the influence of a young colleague named David Mall. Alexander was eventually baptized in the Mediterranean Sea off the coast of Libya. David went on to pastor on the Metro New York District while Alexander moved back to Pakistan. The Metro New York District assisted both financially and by providing training for Alexander to be ordained. Today the work of the church in Pakistan has made remarkable progress, and Alexander serves as the district superintendent.

In India, the work took several significant forward steps. Perhaps the greatest of these during my tenure as regional director was the beginning of South Asia Nazarene Bible College (SANBC).

Our previous work in this country stretched back over 100 years and was located in a confined rural area of Maharashtra State in central India. This constitutes the oldest mission field in the Church of the Nazarene. In this area was a Bible college, which had begun in 1936. It was small, rural, and trained young men from rural areas, all of whom spoke the local language of this area.

In 1994 we decided to close this school and

begin a process that would lead to a decentralized educational approach for the whole of South Asia. This meant organizing classes in many languages, which, in turn, meant developing new curriculum and writing or translating materials in many languages. It was a massive project, and primary responsibility for constructing the new school was given to Rev. John Haines who served as the regional education coordinator. He spent thousands of hours on this undertaking and visited India many times.

Today almost 1,500 students study courses in 12 languages and three countries with about 90 centers of learning. The first graduates are now in ministry, and an increasing number of graduates will be prepared each year.

The period of time between Berlin in 1989 and Baghdad in 2004 was a unique, jam-packed, eventful span. It was filled with earth-shattering events, turbulent crises, changing boundaries, wars and rumors of wars, and vast new vistas of opportunity for the church.

But in between all the meetings, the boards, the committees, the study groups, the strategy sessions, the district assemblies, and the staff meetings came the people. At the end of the day, it was the people who made the difference.

Out of the hundreds of Nazarene leaders I could write about, my space is limited to only a few. I hope these stories give you a feel for the people who make up the Church of the Nazarene in Eurasia.

Nikolaj Sawatzky

Nikolaj and Lydia studied at European Nazarene College (EuNC) in Switzerland, having emigrated from different parts of the Soviet Union but both having a German heritage. While at EuNC they joined the Church of the Nazarene. In time Nikolaj became the Russia radio coordinator and litera-ture coordi-nator. In the early days he

Lydia and Nikolaj Sawatzky

was the only native Russian language speaker with theological training to translate and interpret texts and the theological message. Nikolaj and Lydia are now Nazarene missionaries.

Abdo Khanashat

Abdo is a layman from Beirut, Lebanon. He has served as principal of the Nazarene school in Beirut, and during the 17 years of civil war, which nearly destroyed the country of Lebanon, Abdo held the work together. He kept the school open and maintained the financial records of the district while encouraging the maintenance of denominational work. He is a godly man, tested under fire (and bombs), and is a hero of the faith.

Sunil Dandge

Sunil comes from a rural area in India. His father and mother worked for the Nazarene mission

Sunil Dandge

for years, so Sunil grew up knowing the church and Christ. When Nazarene work in Calcutta was begun by missionaries John and Doris Anderson, this great city needed Indian leadership. John asked Sunil and his wife, Sarah, if they would leave their home, family, and language to move to a large and difficult city, learn a new language, and begin our work. It was the kind of sacrifice we attribute to missionaries. Sunil and Sarah agreed, and in time Sunil became district superintendent of the East India District and presently serves as president of South Asia Nazarene Bible College.

Andrei and Svetlana Khobnia

Andrei and Svetlana are from Volgograd (formerly Stalingrad) in southern Russia. They discovered the Church of the Nazarene in the early days of our existence in their country. Mentored by missionaries Chuck and Carla Sunberg, the Khobnias began a journey into pastoral ministry and teaching that has led them today into a doctoral program at Nazarene Theological College in Manchester, England. They both completed graduate work at Nazarene Theological Seminary (NTS) in Kansas City, and serve as models of many young Russian leaders of the church.

Vinay Gaikwad

Vinay is a preacher's kid from India. His father was district superintendent for many years. In time Vinay traveled to the United States to secure his graduate theology degree at NTS, then returned to India to pastor. Today he shepherds a large church in a city northwest of Mumbai, India. He represents thousands of young pastors who carry on the work of the church in South Asia.

Billy Mitchell

Billy, who passed away in 2006, was part of the paramilitary establishment in Northern Ireland. He fought the Catholic groups with fanatic zeal, and was eventually convicted of murder and imprisoned for life by the British government. Billy accepted Christ in prison, and a miraculous turn of events allowed for his release after several years. He and his wife soon discovered the Church of the Nazarene. His passion was to start a reconciliation ministry for ex-convicts on both sides of the Protestant/Catholic divide. This eventually became possible by a grant of money from Nazarene Compassionate Ministries. Hundreds of former paramilitary convicts have been reconciled, trained, and nurtured back into society through this ministry.

Khalil Halaseh

Khalil is a young pastor in Amman, Jordan. Since Khalil has been pastor, his church is crowded out for worship services, which are a celebration of joy in Christ. He has been into Iraq many times preaching the gospel and now helps nurture young leaders for ministry throughout the Middle East. In fact, out of a group of young Iraqi men he was discipling emerged pastors who, in 2002 and later, began to filter back into Iraq to plant the Church of the Nazarene. Dynamic and communicative, Brother Khalil is representative of pastors throughout the Nazarene Arabic-speaking world who spread the light and salt of the gospel wherever they go.

Conclusion

I think of the Eurasia Region as the most amazing piece of real estate in the world. It is filled with billions of people. It encompasses thousands of years of history. It has been the home of the world's primary religions, political philosophies, and social theories. It has proven to be one of the most difficult areas for ministry in the 20th century.

And yet, in the midst of the storm, God is doing surprising things in these surprising places. And the story continues on.

BEYOND BAGHDAD
The Continuation of the
Work in Eurasia

DR. GUSTAVO CROCKER

What would a young Guatemalan architect do in such a vast and complex missionary environment as the Eurasia Region? Would the church in Europe easily accept the leadership of someone who is not one of them? How would someone who has been working in the pan-evangelical world fit back into leading the missionary enterprise of a large portion of his denomination?

These questions, and many others, ran through my mind and the minds of many others when the announcement of my election as regional director was made. It is easy to become skeptical about leadership changes, especially when the unexpected happens to be in center stage. Thus the story of my calling to Eurasia becomes relevant.

In early February of 2003, the imminence of the war in Iraq beckoned evangelical Christians to help the scores of people trapped in the middle of the conflict. As senior vice-president for programs at the World Relief Corporation of the National Association of Evangelicals, I had been given the task to work with a coalition of evangelical European agencies by facilitating the response of western evangelicals to those displaced by the war.

With that assignment, I joined my European colleagues in a small town in Denmark and then traveled to Jordan. While the project ended up being a successful demonstration of the love of Christ from evangelicals all over the world, I didn't know this trip was to prepare my heart for the most exciting and challenging assignment of my ministry so far.

February in Denmark is very cold. It is even colder for a tropical Guatemalan like me. When I arrived and stepped off the train, hoping to catch a taxi to the hotel, I realized a winter storm had hit the area. The streets were empty. The only option was to drag my luggage nearly five blocks in the bitter cold.

I finally made it to the hotel. After a long, hot shower I was ready for dinner. As I sat by myself in this pristine European hotel restaurant, I looked at two elderly couples in the restaurant—the only other people in the place. I also looked out the window and saw the beautiful, well-preserved buildings of this typical Danish town.

"What if I called you to this part of the world?" I heard a Voice inside me ask. I laughed. *"No, really,"* the Voice persisted. *"Would you come to this part of*

the world that is so beautiful and yet so cold to My voice?"

Ten months later, I received a call from Dr. Bustle, director of World Mission. "The votes are in and the General Board has confirmed your election as regional director for the Eurasia Region," he said. It was not as cold as that February evening in Denmark, but I felt as shocked by this phone call as I was by the lonely conversation in the small Danish hotel back in February. Next thing I know, my family and I are living in Europe and serving with a beautiful host of Nazarene Christians.

I also didn't know that my February trip to Jordan following my visit in Denmark would result in the establishment of the Church of the Nazarene in Iraq. The coalition I was working with ended up with two main projects to help displaced Iraqis. In one of those, the Jordanian Evangelical Committee on Relief and Development—of which the Church of the Nazarene was a charter member—sent Arab Christians to rebuild schools and help families cope with the agony of war. By the end of 2003, a Nazarene volunteer had joined the team in northern Iraq and began a Bible study. In Baghdad, several returning refugees had developed a series of contacts and established one congregation and several preaching and prayer points. The seed that had been planted in early 2003 was already bearing fruit.

Initial Harvest

My family and I arrived in Europe in the summer of 2004. Full of expectations and dreams, we soon realized the harvest was indeed plenty.

During my first six months in the office I had the privilege of approving the organization of the first Church of the Nazarene in Iraq. That was soon followed by the second and then the third. In South Asia, I saw God help the Church of the Nazarene develop a system of multiplication sparked by Compassionate Ministries and the *JESUS* film, which was then consolidated by our educational system. I was reminded of what the apostle Paul wrote to the Corinthians: "What, after all, is Apollos? And what is Paul? Only servants, through whom you came to believe—as the Lord has assigned to each his task. I planted the seed, Apollos watered it, but God made it grow" (1 Cor. 3:5-6).

Building Upon a Solid Foundation

My predecessor, Dr. Franklin Cook, is known as one of the finest missiologists in the denomination. I must admit, following him was no easy task. However, it was a blessing to realize he and his team had been working steadily to build a solid foundation so the growth we envisioned could take place. This foundation had several important elements: a clearly articulated and widely owned mission statement; a team of competent, committed missionaries and local leaders; and a soil that was ready for planting.

Dr. Cook's team worked nearly five years to finalize a mission statement that accurately reflects the heart of the International Church of the Nazarene both globally and in Eurasia. This meticulous work resulted in one of the finest statements for a missions agency today. Understanding that our global mission is "to make Christlike disciples in the nations," the mission statement for the Eurasia Region is "to develop an indigenous, self-supported, interdependent, holiness church in the Wesleyan-Arminian tradition."

This summarizes what the Church of the Nazarene in Eurasia is all about: church development—but not just any kind of church development. The missionary enterprise in Eurasia is about developing Nazarene churches that can support and reproduce themselves. We desire churches that—within the context of their social, political, and religious realities—embrace and teach our doctrine of heart holiness from a solid historical and biblical tradition.

Casting the Vision: The Regional Strategy

When I arrived in Eurasia, our mission statement was the compass that provided direction to the work in the region. My next step was to organize a group of leaders to help me articulate the vision of the church in Eurasia for years to come. The result was a statement that is clear, comprehensive, and compelling: "transforming our world . . . in Christ, like Christ, for Christ."

This vision—congruent with our denominational core values of a Christian, holiness, and missional church—will be seen through:

- Unity of identity, integration of all ministries, and coherence of direction as the Church of the Nazarene in our various contexts and cultures (John 17; core values of the Church of the Nazarene).
- Evangelism and church planting that focuses on building the church and maximizing resources as appropriate.
- Discipleship of people of all ages as a major focus in all our efforts (Eph. 4:12-13).
- A church that intentionally ministers to and involves children and youth.
- All churches, districts, and ministries in the region healthy and growing toward maturity and holism (Luke 2:52).
- Missionaries in the region whose priority and focus is the timely handover of the work to a maturing, indigenous church (Rom. 15:23; Col. 1:24-29).
- Eurasian Nazarenes involved in operations,

representation, leadership, and ministries at the regional and global levels of the Church of the Nazarene.

- A church where prayer is central to the life and ministry of every congregation.

Strategic Priorities

With that vision in mind, the leadership of the region prayerfully considered the strategic priorities of the church for the future. Early in 2005, the regional strategy committee met to process the vision and the ministry requirements for its implementation. We needed to put wheels in motion if we wanted the vision to be more than just a slogan or a series of good intentions. The committee helped us define our ministry priorities for the future. The resulting statement reads:

"Embedded in prayer, we believe that this vision will be accomplished by focusing on the following strategic priorities:

- Make effective evangelism and discipleship central to our efforts.
- Facilitate programs and resources to evangelize and mobilize children and youth.
- Define and develop healthy churches, districts, and ministries.
- Focus on planting healthy and sustainable churches that reproduce.

- Emphasize leadership development, training, and education.
- Integrate compassionate ministries in our work."

During our first years of ministry we placed all our energy into making these strategic priorities a reality in all levels of the region. I pray for the day when I can write about the results of these strategic plans. In the meantime, I would like to share some snapshots of vision fulfillment already happening in Eurasia.

Results of the Harvest

God has blessed His vision for us in Eurasia, and we are already seeing growth—both in quantity and quality. The growth in numbers has been coupled with sustained development efforts in all fields and institutions of the region. Our new works are experiencing qualified leaders while our older works continue to find new ways to engage current generations for ministry. During my visits to the various fields of the region, I have the opportunity to meet scores of mature leaders and laypeople committed to reaching their lands for Christ. What this means is the work of our theological education institutions is bearing fruit. We foresee increasing numbers of believers discipled into holiness and influencing their communities for Christ.

IN TERMS OF NUMERIC GROWTH, THE EURASIA REGION HAS EXPERIENCED DOUBLE-DIGIT GROWTH EVERY YEAR SINCE 2003.

In terms of numeric growth, the Eurasia Region has experienced double-digit growth every year since 2003. The average growth of 14 percent in the last five years is among the largest in World Mission areas. Since 2003, the region has had a net gain of 39,000 members (nearly 35 percent of the membership of the denomination in Eurasia has been added between 2003 and 2006) and 722 newly organized churches. By the end of 2006, we had 1,641 organized churches and 505 preaching points for a total of 2,146 congregations.

Nearly one-third of all the organized churches in Eurasia have been organized in the last four years—the making of a true movement. In 2006 alone we organized an average of one new church per day and ordained an average of one elder each week. Our theological education institutions have reported a steady student enrollment, with a total of 374 residential students and 1,445 extension students receiving 104 degrees, diplomas, and certificates. Even though these figures constitute considerable progress, growth on some of the fields still requires a larger number of leaders.

God at Work in South Asia

Thanks to the *JESUS* film, Nazarene Compassionate Ministries, and the "Each One Win One" strategy, Nazarenes in South Asia have doubled since the year 2000. The current pace of growth is such that they are planting nearly five new preaching points a day. One out of five preaching points becomes a fully organized church in an average of three years, so they have organized an average of 350 churches per year between 2003 and 2006. Their goal, however, is even higher. Nazarenes in South Asia have had the vision to organize 1,500 new congregations by 2010.

Like in the Book of Acts, numeric growth requires new workers for the harvest. By the end of 2006 more than 2,000 students enrolled in extension education classes in more than 30 centers around the field. In May 2006 we graduated the first 72 graduates of the South Asia Nazarene Bible College.

Bangladesh is perhaps the best example of God's hand at work in South Asia. Originally started through Nazarene Compassionate Ministries, the Church of the Nazarene in Bangladesh has grown from two congregations in 1994 to a district of 502 organized churches in 2006. The secret of the work has been holism, passion, persistence, and organization.

I met the deputy prime minister for nongovernmental organizations in one of my visits to Bangladesh in 1996. Nazarene Compassionate Ministries was known in Bangladesh for the thoroughness of its programs. This national leader told me that, even though they knew we were a religious group, the most important thing was that we were helping the people who needed assistance the most. Nazarene Compassionate Ministries was working, and continues to work today, with the poorest people in one of the poorest nations in the world, and it does so holistically.

Renewal in Southern Europe

Traditionally Catholic, southern Europe hasn't been favorable to open expressions of evangelicalism on its soil. As hard as the soil may be, however, the Church of the Nazarene has found a ministry niche that is giving us a most-needed presence in this part of the region. This is our work among immigrant communities.

Ministering to the immigrant has proven to be an effective strategy for reaching dormant communities. Like in the times of the Early Church, immigrant communities in southern Europe are sensitive to receiving and sharing Christ with the mainstream culture. Most of our churches in Spain, Portugal, and France are immigrant churches. However, as the next generation is ministered to in bicultural ways, these second-generation immigrant Nazarenes have become the stable presence of Christian holiness in their communities. As a result, we have seen new works and growth in all countries in this area of the region. In Portugal, thanks to their indigenous leadership, the Church of the Nazarene has experienced three consecutive years of growth after more than a decade of losses. Spain marked their 25th anniversary by doubling the number of churches between 2002 and 2007. And in France, perhaps the hardest soil of all in southern Europe, the Church of the Nazarene has started two new self-supporting congregations with national pastors since the year 2000.

Church Planting in Northern Europe and the Middle East

Christianity in northern Europe—the crib of Protestantism and Wesleyanism—has been on a steady decline. In the Middle East, Christianity grows under the most difficult and risky circumstances. In the midst of such somber environments, the Church of the Nazarene continues fulfilling its vision of transformation.

In the Northern Europe field, the Church of the Nazarene has focused its energy on church-planting initiatives. In 2006 the leadership of the British Isles districts, Nazarene Theological College in Manches-

The Nazarene congregation in Oslo

ter, and the Eurasia Region partnered to begin the Center for Evangelism and Church Development— an initiative to foster growth and development in the British Isles. Already districts in the British Isles report of new church plants in Northern Ireland, Scotland, and England.

Once again ministry to immigrants proved to be an effective strategy for establishing our presence in difficult ministry locations. After years of considering the expansion of our work in Scandinavia beyond Denmark, the Church of the Nazarene was able to begin in Norway through the work of Rev. Jorge Barros, a Nazarene from the Cape Verde Islands. The first Church of the Nazarene in Oslo was organized in the fall of 2006. It is now a vibrant congregation ministering in English, Spanish, and Portuguese.

Thanks to the work of Rev. Ricardo Romero, a disciple of Dr. Bruno Radi in Argentina, the Church of the Nazarene planted and organized its first work in the French-speaking portion of Switzerland. In July 2007 a second immigrant congregation was organized in Lausanne, Switzerland. The plans are for five more ministry points among both the French and Spanish speakers in the area.

In the Middle East the Church of the Nazarene continues delivering the message of salvation in Christ in spite of persecution and danger. In Iraq—thanks to the leadership of Arab Christians from Jordan—three congregations have been organized, and the gospel is still being preached in the midst of the civil strife.[1] In Jordan, indigenous leaders have taken upon themselves the challenge to establish new works both in the northern and southern regions of the country. After years of consolidating the existing work in the country, Nazarenes in Jordan have planted and organized three new congregations since 2005, and their plans include ministry to Moab and to the Bedouin communities in the area.

Compassion Evangelism in the CIS

When missionaries in Ukraine began searching for the best way to do ministry in this country, they

Bob Skinner, field strategy coordinator for the CIS field, and his wife, Colleen

seemed to hit a wall. Most of the traditional church-planting efforts took longer than expected, and the results were barely sustainable. Through prayer and community interaction, Rev. Bob Skinner—missionary district superintendent to Ukraine—soon began to see a better way of responding to the needs of the people: through recovery programs. Alcoholism and drug addiction are prevalent in all levels of society in this part of the world. With this in mind, the Church of the Nazarene opened a rehabilitation center for victims of alcohol and drug abuse. The result was dozens of converts who not only committed themselves to a better life, but also to preaching the liberating gospel that had released them. Many of those individuals planted new churches and became catalyst leaders for entire areas of the country. Today, thanks to this God-given vision, there are more than 35 churches in Ukraine. The plans are to plant at least 5 new churches per year. A new generation of workers is growing, and the rehabilitation and revival ministries continue.

Isaiah-Caleb Project

I had been in office for just over a month when

I traveled to Italy to meet Dr. Bruno Radi and Dr. Louie Bustle to explore the possibility of a new church plant in Bruno's hometown of Pedazzo.

Having worked together in the past, our conversation turned to the struggle of keeping Latin American young adults involved in Nazarene missions. "We are losing our youth to parachurch organizations," Bruno said. "We need to do something to keep our young adults engaged in Nazarene missions, and we need to do it now," he added. My time working with missionary mobilization for other agencies globally helped give us the background we needed to shape a vision.

The discussion resulted in the Isaiah-Caleb Project, developed by the Eurasia Region and presented to Bruno Radi and Christian Sarmiento (directors at the time for the South America Region and the Mexico and Central America Region) who embraced and supported it. The idea was to mobilize Latin American young adults to serve as volunteers in places like Italy, Spain, and Portugal—the lands of their ancestors—or in the Middle East, where Latin Americans find it easier to blend in ethnically and culturally.

The Isaiah-Caleb Project provides a way for South and Central America to send missionaries—a new development for global Nazarene missions. Initially these individuals are assigned in small groups

One of the Caleb teams

to a specific hosting church or district with the purpose of serving as catalytic church planters. The central task of these volunteers is to establish cell groups and plant new churches alongside current work in the hosting countries. In turn, these young volunteers may return to Latin America with a new perspective on missions that will help develop the new generation of leaders for the Church of the Nazarene in Latin America.

In May 2007 I had the privilege of being in Guatemala to receive, on behalf of the Eurasia Region, the first class of short-term missionaries from Latin America. After three years of preparation, Eurasia welcomed 13 individuals: 4 to Italy, 6 to Spain, and 3 to the Middle East. These young volunteers are on the ground working in partner teams to aid in the evangelism and church planting of the local host churches.

Scott Armstrong from the Mexico and Central America (MAC) Region said, "This is not only going to change Eurasia, it's going to change MAC, it's going to change SAM [the South America Region], it's going to change our whole environment for missions. These people are going to come back and say, 'This was not what I had expected, but the Lord was with me.' I'm so excited about it."

The Future: In God's hands

I am again in Denmark. This time my wife and I are en route to Oslo, Norway, where the First Church of the Nazarene has organized an International Festival, and I have been invited to be the preacher. It is a cold summer morning, and I can see outside the window of my hotel room. The place is beautiful, pristine, cozy, inviting. It is still as beautiful in the summer as it was in the winter four years ago.

There are few people on the streets. I guess it is so quiet and tranquil that people do not seem to feel the need for anything—including Christ. But they do need Christ! I can see it in the way young people look at me, as if they are content but not happy. I can see it in the way churches have become just one of the institutions responsible for "religious affairs" in most towns.

When I was in Denmark four years ago, I was on my way to Jordan to plan for the work of Christians in response to the Iraqi war. At the time of this writing, the conflict still continues. The world has changed since the events of 2003, including the fact that the Church of the Nazarene now has a church in Baghdad. And while I don't know what lies beyond Baghdad, I do know Jesus told us, "I will build my church, and the gates of Hades will not overcome it" (Matt. 16:18).

I will meet tomorrow with the district superintendent of the Scandinavian District. We will pray together. We will continue dreaming dreams about the future of the church in Scandinavia and in Eurasia. We will celebrate each fruit (like the church in Oslo) as much as we celebrate the harvest-by-combine in South Asia. And we will leave the future of Eurasia in God's hands. It always has been in His hands, and it always will be.

NOTES

1. When this chapter was written, one of the pastors in Iraq had to flee the country due to personal threats against him and his family. Two other pastors are facing dangerous circumstances, yet the church continues its ministry to scores of Iraqi families.

CALL TO ACTION

1. Visit the Eurasia Region's web site at www.eurasianazarene.org to learn more about the exciting things God is doing in this part of the world. While you are there, take a look at the latest prayer requests for the region and spend time lifting them before the Lord in prayer.

2. Subscribe to the Eurasia Region's monthly e-newsletter *Where Worlds Meet* by e-mailing the editor at whereworldsmeet@eurasianazarene.org. Each issue contains greetings from a different field; the latest news on people, events and ministries throughout the region; and information about upcoming events and prayer needs.

3. Pray for Dr. Crocker and the many other leaders and pastors across this great region. Pray for God to impart His wisdom, guidance, and discernment in every decision they face.

4. Consider volunteering your time in one of the many ministries in the Eurasia Region. For more information, contact the regional office at office@eurasiaregion.org or visit their web site.

PRONUNCIATION GUIDE

Preface
Schofield   SKOHW-feeld

Chapter 1
Benvenue   ben-ven-EW
Büsingen   BEW-zeeng-gen
Madeira   muh-DEE-rah
Zwingli   ZWEENG-lee

Chapter 2
Bonn   BAHN
Cor Holleman   KOHR HAH-luh-muhn
Dekan   dee-KAHN
Evangelisch   ee-van-GE-lish
Haarlem   HAHR-luhm
Miep   MEEP

Chapter 3
Ammari   uh-MAR-ee
Dahs   DAHS
Dinakaran   di-nuh-KAH-rehn
Escudo   is-KEW-doh
Gaikwad   gai-KWAHD
Ingle   EENG-guhl
Karak   kuh-RAHK
Makram Bessada   mah-KRAHM beh-SAW-duh
Mosteller   MAHS-teh-ler
Singh   SEENG

Chapter 4

Abdo Khanashat	ahb-DOH kah-nah-SHAHT
Andrei and Svetlana Khobnia	AHN-drey and svet-LAH-nuh kohb-NEE-uh
Amman	uh-MAHN
Gschwandtner	guh-SHVAHNT-ner
Khalil Halaseh	kuh-LEEL huh-LAH-seh
Li Fuamui	LEE few-AH-mwee
Maharashtra	mah-hah-RAHSH-trah
Maldives	MAHL-deevz
Mumbai	MUHM-bai
Nikolaj Sawatzky	NIK-oh-lai suh-VAHT-skee
Stalingrad	STAH-lin-grad
Sukumal Biswas	soo-koo-MAHL BIZ-wahs
Sunil Dandge	sew-NEEL dan-JEE
Vinay Gaikwad	vee-NAY gai-KWAHD
Volgograd	VOHL-guh-grad
Vollenweider	FOH-len-vei-der

Chapter 5

Bedouin	BEH-doh-win
Cape Verde	KAYP verd
Jorge Barros	HOHR-hay BAH-rohs
Lausanne	lew-ZAHN
Pedazzo	puh-DAZ-oh
Radi	RAH-dee
Ricardo Romero	ri-KAHR-doh roh-MAIR-oh